Out and About at the Dairy Farm

Field Trips

Written by Andy Murphy • Illustrated by Anne McMullen

Content Adviser: Dr. Drew Conroy
Associate Professor of Applied Animal Science, University of New Hampshire, Durham, New Hampshire

Reading Adviser: Lauren A. Liang, M.A.
Literacy Education, University of Minnesota, Minneapolis, Minnesota

PICTURE WINDOW BOOKS
Minneapolis, Minnesota

To my family for their love and support, and especially to my parents, who thought a Guernsey cow would make a good pet. They were right. —A.M.

The author wishes to thank:
- Phyllis, Analesa, Beth, Sharon, and Louise Harvey of Applehurst Farm in Epping, New Hampshire.
- Drew Conroy, Ph.D., Associate Professor of Applied Animal Science at the University of New Hampshire's Thompson School of Applied Science.
- Lynn Garland, 4-H expert and University of New Hampshire cooperative extension educator.

Designer: Melissa Voda
Page production: Picture Window Books
The illustrations in this book were rendered using watercolor and ink.

Picture Window Books
1710 Roe Crest Drive
North Mankato, MN 56003
www.capstonepub.com

Library of Congress Cataloging-in-Publication Data
Murphy, Andy, 1954–
  Out and about at the dairy farm / written by Andy Murphy ; illustrated by Anne McMullen.
    p. cm.
  Summary: Discusses the activities of a dairy farm, describing the machines used and the process used to get the milk to our table.
  ISBN-13: 978-1-4048-0038-0 (hardcover)
  ISBN-10: 1-4048-0038-7 (hardcover)
  ISBN-13: 978-1-4048-0166-0 (paperback)
  ISBN-10: 1-4048-0166-9 (paperback)
  1. Dairy cattle—Juvenile literature. 2. Cows—Juvenile literature. [1. Dairy farms. 2. Dairying. 3. Dairy cattle. 4. Cows.] I. McMullen, Anne, ill. II. Title.
  SF208 .M87 2003
  636.2'142—dc21
                                                                    2002006292

We're going on a field trip to a dairy farm.
We can't wait!

Things to find out:
How do you get milk out of a cow?
Can any cow be milked?
How much milk can you get out of one cow?
Why do cows chew all the time?

Welcome to Red Oak Dairy Farm. We make sure you
have milk for your cereal and ice cream for your cone.
Can you think of anything else made from milk?

At a dairy farm, cows, or female cattle, are raised to produce milk. Some dairy farms have bulls, or male cattle. Farms also have calves, or baby cattle.

Here's a Holstein cow. Her black and white spots are like fingerprints. No other cow has spots just like hers. There are many kinds of milking cows, but we raise Holsteins because they produce the most milk.

A cow can't make milk until she has a baby. Most cows are two years old when they have their first calf. After that, cows have a baby every year, and they continue to give milk. A healthy milk cow gives milk about 10 months out of every year.

A pregnant cow stops giving milk two months before
her calf is born. During this time, she is called a dry cow.
Once her calf is born, she will produce milk again.
These dry cows are on vacation in the meadow.
They eat grass and drink water all day.

8

Cows need more than grass and water to make the best milk. We grow corn for them, too. We mix the corn with grass to make silage, which is cow food.

Cows have a special stomach that helps them eat foods like grass and hay. Cows chew their food a bit and swallow it. Later, they cough it up and chew it some more. This food is called cud. Cows that look like they are chewing gum are really chewing their cud.

A milking cow can eat up to 100 pounds (45 kilograms) of food a day. That's more than most of you weigh.

A milking cow spends most of her time in the barn. She needs plenty of food and water.

After calves are born, they stay with their mothers for a few hours. Then we move the female calves into their own pens in the calf barn. We sell the male calves to farmers who raise them as bulls.

Right after her calf is born, the mother cow produces thick, yellow milk. This milk is the calf's first food. It helps the calf grow strong and protects the calf against germs.

We always put booties over our shoes so we don't carry germs into the milking parlor. Then it's milking time. First we squeeze a bit of milk from the cow. Next we wash and dry the udder. Then we attach the milking machine. This may look scary, but don't worry— it doesn't hurt the cow.

When the milk is pumped out it travels through a tube to a cooling tank.
Holstein cows give enough milk to fill as many as 100 glasses of milk a day.

17

After the cows are milked, we wash their udders
with medicine to protect the cows from germs.
Then the cows walk through a footbath.

18

The footbath has special medicine in it to keep cows' feet healthy.
Cows need healthy feet to get up and down from the milking area.

19

That's the end of our tour. Now that you know about dairy farming, maybe someday you'll come and work with us. Thanks for visiting. Come back anytime.

UDDERLY EASY ICE CREAM

What you need

1 tablespoon (14 grams) sugar

1/2 cup (118 milliliters) whole milk

1/2 teaspoon (2 milliliters) vanilla

4 tablespoons (57 grams) salt

1 small, sandwich-size, zippered freezer bag

1 large zippered freezer bag

ice cubes

towel

an adult to help you

What you do

1. Mix the sugar, milk, and vanilla together in a bowl.

2. Pour the mixture into the small freezer bag. Zip the bag shut, pressing out the extra air.

3. Fill the large freezer bag halfway full of ice cubes.

4. Add the salt to the large bag.

5. Place the small bag inside the large bag. Zip the large bag shut, pressing out the extra air.

6. Wrap the large bag in a towel.

7. Shake for 5 to 10 minutes, or until the milk mixture hardens.

8. Open the large bag and remove the small bag.

9. Wipe the small bag dry, open it, and enjoy the ice cream inside.

FUN FACTS

- A cow has four parts to its stomach. This allows it to eat food that doesn't break down easily.

- Cows don't have top front teeth. They have a tough pad of skin instead. Their long, rough tongues are perfect for tearing grass from the ground.

- Cows must drink 2 gallons (7.6 liters) of water for every 1 gallon (3.8 liters) of milk they produce.

- Before milking machines were invented in 1894, farmers milked cows by hand. They could milk only six cows an hour by hand. With machines, farmers can milk up to 100 cows an hour.

- The end of a cow's tail is called a switch. A cow uses the switch to swat flies from its back.

- A group of 12 or more cows is known as a flink.

- A milking Holstein produces about 115 pounds (52 kilograms) of manure every day.

- A full udder holds 4 to 6 gallons (15 to 23 liters) of milk.

WORDS TO KNOW

bulls—male cattle

calves—cattle that are less than a year old

cattle—animals raised for dairy products or beef

cows—female cattle that have had one or more babies

cud—food that has been partly chewed, swallowed, and coughed up to chew again

dry cows—pregnant cows that are not producing milk

manure—farm animal waste. Manure is often used to enrich the soil.

silage—food for cows made from corn mixed with grass

udder—a baglike pouch on a cow's body in which the cow produces milk

TO LEARN MORE

At the Library

Brady, Peter. Cows. Mankato, Minn.: Bridgestone Books, 1996.

Cooper, Elisha. Ice Cream. New York: Greenwillow Books, 2002.

Gibbons, Gail. The Milk Makers. New York: Aladdin Books, 1999.

Hughes, Sarah. My Dad Works on a Farm. New York: Children's Press, 2001.

On the Web

FactHound offers a safe, fun way to find Web site related to this book.

All of the sites on FactHound have been researched by our staff.

1. Visit www.facthound.com

2. Type in this special code: 1404800387

3. Click on the FETCH IT button.

Your trusty FactHound will fetch the best sites for you!

INDEX